**pearlcatchers**

Fusion – developing your learning organisation

Ignite your Managers and Leaders

Help your people **Flourish** with personal growth and well-being

Let **Praxis** bring drama-enhanced learning and assessment to life

For more information on our CPD Programme, please contact
Sharon M Young
Director / Lead Consultant
01753 670187 / 07973 710228
Or sharon@pearlcatchers.co.uk

1

Permissions may be sought directly from DAW Ltd. via the website www.daw.co.uk

Illustrations purchased from 123RF; cartoons purchased from IMSI, Canada.

Printed and bound in the USA by IngramSpark™

This publication is written to offer suggestions on self-improvement and how to approach your continuing professional development, not to do your CPD for you. While self-help, it is not a substitute for the advice of your doctor, lawyer, accountant, or any of your advisors, personal or professional, nor does it substitute the regulations governing your profession in your territory.

The legal bit: No responsibility is assumed by the author for any injury and/or damage to persons or property as a matter of products liability, negligence or otherwise, or from any use or operation of any methods, products, instructions or ideas contained in the material herein.

If you would like further information about DAW Ltd., our CPD products and services, our Learning & Development tools and techniques, or our Mentoring Programme, please call our UK office [+44 (0)1295 76 86 06] during usual business hours or search online for www.daw-cpd.com

Mackay, Adrian 1955 – Author

Master your CPD – *in 3 minutes a day*

ISBN 978-1-9995945-0-3

THANKS TO THE CREATIVE TEAM

You have been the creative inspiration behind this book – so thank you!

Well, people just like you: professional people in jobs, as employers and as employees. Inspiration has come from my former managers and my staff, my clients, and those delegates on the thousands of professional training courses I have delivered or attended over the past 40 years.

As a tutor on the Chartered Management Institute Certificate and Diploma courses, through attending classes myself as a delegate at Oxford College of Marketing, at Northampton University, attending my MBA classes at Hull University Business School, and working with the Chartered Institute of Marketing, tutoring at St Gallen Business School in Switzerland, and in delivering professional development workshops as far apart as Manhattan and Dubai, Istanbul and Lagos in Nigeria, as a sports coach and RFU Referee in rugby, I have noticed an enduring theme when it comes to study, work and play – wherever one looks, people love to do things successfully.

I wrote this book to share my findings and to help you do your thing successfully, too.

This book would not have started without the guide from Peter Thomson and his team.

This book would not be finished without the splendid efforts of my creative wife, Jan.

Thank you all.

Mac

MASTER YOUR CPD

... *in 3 minutes a day*

*Featuring the 7 critical mistakes
to avoid with your CPD*

*The surprisingly simple system
to master your
Continuing Professional Development
to progress your career
– and reap the rewards you deserve*

Adrian 'Mac' Mackay

BSc(Hons) DipM MCIM DipDigM CMkr PCertM CMgr MCMI MBA

CONTENTS

MASTER YOUR CPD

So, you get your teeth checked by a dentist? Maybe once or twice a year? Well done!

Sadly, your teeth are still likely to decay and fall out – unless you brush them twice a day!

It is the same with CPD. If you do it once a year – just before your deadline – you could be in trouble... and it hurts.

Record your CPD on day 365 only if you can remember what you learnt each day since day one. If you can, then good luck to you.

But that is not very professional. It's no fun – and I've tried it. Once...

So, for the rest of us, you have the solution in your hand. In this book you'll discover it takes just three minutes a day – a bit like cleaning your teeth.

Yes, as it is 3 mins. a day. That's 15 mins. a week... an hour a month, 12 hours a year.

But, I bet you do more than 12 hours a year – I know some professionals currently have to (accountants, barristers, dentists, vets and doctors) and some no defined hours (solicitors and managers).

Sure, you go on courses – but there are lots of other ways you learn. You do some fun things, every day. And it doesn't have to be painful to keep track of it.

Let me show you how...

CHAPTER ONE

PERSPECTIVE – WHAT IS CPD?

The clue is in the title: 'CPD' is your on-going (**continuing**) job-related (**professional**) improvement (**development**).

Let's take a look at a definition of **CPD**: *Intentionally developing the knowledge, skills and personal competence needed to perform professional responsibilities.*

What, for you, is the most important word in that definition?

Some might say *'responsibilities'*. As a professional you have responsibilities – to your employer and those defined by your regulator, industry or professional body to which you belong, and all of us certainly by statute. You also have clients (or patients – if you are a medical professional or vet) and owe a responsibility to them, too.

> *...solicitors must reflect on their practice and undertake regular learning and development so their skills and knowledge remain up to date. (SRA)*

But, while all the words in the definition are important, of course, the most crucial is *'intentionally'*. You do something, which was to you necessary and was planned, to improve your professional competence – and that is what this book is all about.

Another definition:

Competency – *The ability to perform the roles and tasks required by one's job to the expected standard.*

Three things to note here:

1. *'Tasks'* refer to the technical aspects of your job.
2. *'Roles'* may mean that you are a manager of more junior staff in your firm.
3. *'Expected standard'*, perhaps most crucially the definition recognises that there must be some defined level of ability for your job role and the tasks within that.

Now, a competency has **breadth**: defining *a range of skill-sets across a core competency.*

Are you below 'par'?

You might, for example, expect a professional to be able to *'communicate clearly and effectively'*. Hands up – can you? Well of course you can. But the skill-set can be divided thus:

A professional:

- *Ensures that communication achieves its intended objective*
- *Responds to and addresses individual characteristics effectively and sensitively*
- *Uses the most appropriate method and style of communication for the situation and the recipient(s)*
- *Uses clear, succinct and accurate language avoiding unnecessary technical terms*
- *Uses formalities appropriate to the context and purpose of the communication*
- *Maintains the confidentiality and security of communications*
- *Imparts any difficult or unwelcome news clearly and sensitively*

Like me, you'll see that you are probably better at some things than others.

That idea of *'level of ability'* suggests, of course, that the more senior you are, the more complex things you will be expected to handle: so this is another dimension to competence. Hence, competences also have **height**: they get more complex (higher standards) as one makes progress through a career pathway; see Table 1.

A **Competency Framework**, therefore, sets out and defines each individual competency (such as problem-solving or people management) across a whole range of activities required by individuals working in a firm or the profession and defines the competency that is required at a **given level of seniority**.

I'll explain how you can handle the CPD Framework in more detail later.

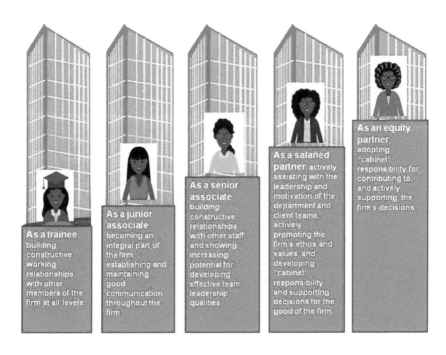

As a trainee, building constructive working relationships with other members of the firm at all levels.

As a junior associate, becoming an integral part of the firm, establishing and maintaining good communication throughout the firm.

As a senior associate building constructive relationships with other staff, and showing increasing potential for developing effective team leadership qualities.

As a salaried partner, actively assisting with the leadership and motivation of the department and client teams, actively promoting the firm's ethos and values, and developing "cabinet" responsibility and supporting decisions for the good of the firm.

As an equity partner, adopting "cabinet" responsibility for, contributing to, and actively supporting, the firm's decisions.

Figure 1. Higher Competency Standards in 'Managing Working Relationhips'

Breadth and height (or depth if you prefer) are the dimensions of competency making a **framework**. Naturally enough, competences grow as you advance your career. So, as you follow a career path, any defined competency will have increasing scale of complexity as you get more senior – which is where CPD comes in.

Making a decision to improve your professionalism in a clearly defined way gives you what you want. Not everyone wants to make Equity Partner but getting better at your job enables you to get involved in more interesting work – and that brings you its own 'lifestyle' rewards. That can mean whatever you want it to – personal to you.

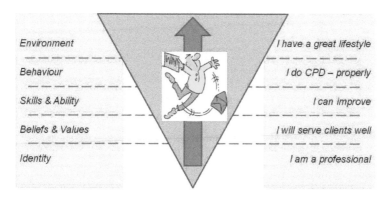

Figure 2. Start at the identity level and get where you want to go

That choice you make is personal to you and starts at the identity level – See figure 1. As you move up the levels you get the lifestyle you want.

If you get a grip on your CPD at the start of your career, how much will that be worth in job enrichment, and career progression – or being able to demonstrate extra value to your current or future employer?

Let's illustrate this by a simple approach:

Suppose your average salary in any given decade is just 10 percent higher because you are able to get a better salary increase or get a better paid job. What effect would that have over your career?

Your Age:	20's	30's	40's	50's	60's
Average annual salary	£30,000	£40,000	£50,000	£60,000	£70,000
10% extra salary	10 x £3,000	10 x x£4,000	10 x £5,000	10 x £6,000	10 x £7,000
Total extra in decade	£30,000	£40,000	£50,000	£60,000	£70,000
Cumulative increase	£30,000	£70,000	£120,000	£180,000	**£250,000**
Your current salary					
10 x 10% extra in decade					
Cumulative increase					

Calculate your numbers and how much extra would you add to your earnings from just three minutes a day working on your CPD?

If all this sounds so wonderful, which of these 7 critical mistakes do you make with your CPD?

CHAPTER TWO

PROBLEMS – THE 7 CRITICAL MISTAKES PROFESSIONALS MAKE

1 "I AM TOO EXPERIENCED / SENIOR"

Some people say, *"I have been doing this job for 20 years. Why do I need CPD?"* The risk is they may have had one year's experience repeated 20 times!

Do you have a mobile phone? How long have you had your current handset? How old is LinkedIn, Twitter, or your firm's intranet? Seen a webinar recently?

You may have spotted that the world of work is changing. Are you keeping up?

As a senior person in your firm, naturally you'll be committed to improving the 'results', whatever they may be. You'll want everyone to do their bit so all can share in that prosperity.

Are you seeing some staff repeat the same old mistakes or are you showing them the way by leading a 'learning organisation'?

2 "I AM WAITING ON HR / THAT COURSE TO RUN AT THE END OF THE YEAR"

You know you should go on that Time Management Course – you just don't have time!

I was like that – so busy with the journey I forgot to smell the flowers en route. Thank goodness I spotted small people crawling around my house – I took them to be my children and thought I should get to know them.

Around that time I met John Wilmshurst who became my business partner (the W of DAW). He taught me so much about getting organised that we found time to co-author three seminal text books for students of marketing and of advertising – I've now written seven. I have also found time to study a new Postgraduate Degree every decade – just for fun.

You don't have to wait for something to happen – especially for your CPD. You are likely to be doing loads of it; it is just about picking it up as you go along.

3 "I DON'T WANT TO – IT IS TOO DIFFICULT"

An enduring theme in this book is our motivation to do something: we either move *away* from something we don't like or *towards* something we do.

Most people will want to move away from the risk of investigation by their professional regulator and avoid being struck off! While mostly true that is hardly inspiring anyone to action – unless it is to avoid a crisis.

So, what is your 'towards motivation' to do some CPD? Get a promotion, a new job, do more interesting stuff? All things are possible – but going on a training course can be difficult:

Attending a CPD training day may mean an even earlier start; making particular arrangements at home; travel on a crowded, unfamiliar route; stress of being late and having it all repeated on the way home. And then you return to a pile of work, plus messages and e-mails in your inbox!

Understandably: too difficult!

But, when it comes to CPD there are at least a dozen other activities that *are* CPD, that you probably do already, and are interesting things to do, too.

And when I tell you all your current CPD can be summarised on two sheets of A4 paper in three minutes a day – that doesn't seem too arduous, now does it?

4 "I CAN'T AFFORD THE MONEY"

A moment's thought: can you afford not to?

- Any litigator will tell you that the cost of defending yourself against an action from your Regulator will be greater than that of avoiding it in the first place – and that's not just the financial cost, either.
- Think of the cost of hiring someone to the same standard as one of your top performers – compared to the modest investment in CPD to help retain your best talent.

But you might be able to earn more – and progressing your career brings many rewards beyond the financial.

"Hello, this is your regulator speaking... about your CPD"

Let's look at it another way. There are a dozen things that are CPD activities – beyond attending a training course; most will not need you to raid the piggy-bank.

Even if you wanted my CPD Tool Kit, stuffed full with enough ideas, support and document masters to run the CPD for your **whole** firm; it will only cost you less than a fiver a week for the whole year[1]. (Go to www.daw-cpd.com and contact us for details).

5 "I FIND TRAINING COURSES BORING"

Death by PowerPoint, dreary presenters, someone reading their notes to you, or pitched way below what you were expecting... we've all been there![2]

That might be because you are selecting training on the wrong criteria. With the approach used in this guide, you'll be able to identify your learning and development (L&D) needs and find the right activity that will engage you – and meet your personal CPD needs.

And note I said learning – attending a training course might be one such option, of course, but again you'll be able to select the right one for you – its level and its accessibility (where and when you can engage with it) to suit you.

6 "I AM NOT SURE WHAT TO DO"

> *"If a person empties their purse into their head,*
> *no one can take it away from them...*
> *...an investment in knowledge*
> *always pays the best interest".*
> **Benjamin Franklin on education**

---

[1] (+VAT if you are in the UK)
[2] Naturally, attending any of my training courses is an entertaining and thoroughly rewarding learning experience – but I am pretty busy and can't be everywhere! My portfolio is coming online so watch out for that!

When it comes to training courses, if the boss or your HR Manager tells you what to do, where to go, and when, life is good. You pitch-up, sit quietly, bring back the notes and your certificate confirms your hours of CPD. It was a day out and you may have got a lunch. Simple – but not particularly effective – and incomplete as CPD, to boot!

And now, more and more, Regulators are looking for 'Outcome Schemes'.[3]

You might be given a 'menu' of courses the firm is putting on for you – so you choose one that seems least boring but is that what you really need?

Now things get complicated. The more choices, the more risk you have that you have made the wrong one.

You can be bamboozled by social media filling every waking hour with information, tips, news, fake news, important stuff and the downright irrelevant.

This is where having a properly structured competency framework to guide you, a simple method of assessing where you are today, and clear options you can take to pursue your L&D – all summarised on two sheets of A4 – is not only quick and simple but also very effective!

---

[3] This is a relatively new development and is utilised heavily within the medical profession. Here, individual professionals must undertake a range of training activities (which may or may not be governed by a set number of hours), but must demonstrate how their learning has impacted their role positively and improved their professional practice. The Solicitors' Regulation Authority has moved to such a scheme since 2016.

Then you can be sure you are not wasting your time and can get on with fee-earning / professional work knowing your CPD is 'on message'!

7 "I FIND CPD IS BUREAUCRATIC / TEDIOUS / I LOST MY RECORDS"

I loathe 'formology' – the study of forms and how to annoy people that have to fill them in!

There is always another form developed by some dear soul to help measure something or another: largely things that suit the measurer – often not the measured.

I have seen:

✘ Bureaucratic nightmares

✘ 12 page documents for annual appraisals: staff called it 'punishment week'

> *"Every doctor is required to demonstrate how they keep up-to-date across their whole scope of work". (GMC)*

✘ CPD Tool-kits containing 'chocolate spanners'

✘ A 33 page 'CPD guide' for CEO's

✘ Generic or 'incompetent' competency frameworks – duplicates, omissions, you name it

✘ Online Learning Management Systems with tiny text fields

While online systems have their merits it is a curious thing; when you put so much effort into typing something it is much harder to delete that effort and start again. We don't handwrite much anymore, I know, and having something online is great.

OK: ignore iffy WiFi access, poor signal strength, system crashes, small screens, forgotten access codes, cyber-crime, etc. it is better than a piece of paper.

Except for one thing: your brain and how it stores information.

Now, I'm not pretending to be a neuro-science guru – I studied it, once, and I know I am not one! However, I did read this, reported from 'A Neuroscientist', Judy Willis, a short while ago[4]:

'Brains evolved to better protect the well-being of its owner and species. One way that this is important for you is that effort and attention are limited commodities so your brain parses out to the actions it predicts will be successful in protection or pleasure.

'So, for example, when you jot something down with a pen, there is a positive emotional response in the brain. Doodles anyone?

'The pleasure of your own creation increases the brain's release of dopamine, a neurotransmitter that increases pleasure, motivation, perseverance through challenges, and resilience to setbacks.

'In addition, there is a beneficial response in your amygdala. The amygdala is a switching station (there's one on each side

---

[4] https://www.nwp.org/cs/public/print/resource/3555 (Accessed May 2018) - Judy Willis, a board-certified neurologist in Santa Barbara, California, attended the UCLA School of Medicine, where she remained as a resident and ultimately became chief resident in neurology.

of your brain) in your brain's emotional-monitoring limbic system that determines if input will go to the reflective, higher cognitive brain (the prefrontal cortex) or down to your reactive, involuntary brain.

'The brain scans of subjects learning in supportive and emotionally pleasurable situations show facilitated passage of information through the amygdala up to the higher cognitive brain, so learning associated with positive emotion is retained longer.'

So, how about two pieces of A4 paper you can create yourself, keep track of your journey, jot down what comes to mind, and have to hand in your desk?

Three minutes a day. That is my promise to you.

After all, I am too lazy or too busy to complicate things. We'll look at these in Chapter 9 ('Proof')...

CHAPTER THREE

PAIN OF PROCRASTINATION – THE LESS I DO THE HARDER IT GETS

"Here is some sound advice", my boss said to me on my first day in international pharmaceutical marketing: *"Do that which makes most money first"*.

So, there is always something that needs to be done in a professional services organisation: another client, a patient, something to sort out as part of your core job as a professional. It is what you do. But do we get dragged into problems that aren't our own? Photocopier on the blink again?

Is this really your job?

But every day most of us learn something new. We just hadn't noticed it – or noted it.

Then I met a wise man, Peter Thompson, who said, "*The day we stop learning is the day we stop earning*". This is because what you learn today will give value to what you learned yesterday.

How much of what you do today – or the way you do it – is the same as when you first set out on your career?

The more you can learn to solve client problems better, use technology smarter, and do more interesting work, the greater will be your quality of life.

Remember your daily teeth brushing? We only put off more pain to a later date by not organising ourselves better today.

So, we all have chores – that's why they are a *chore*!

Leave anything to the last minute and it is painful. And let's face it, there are more interesting things to do than to try to account for what you did 11 months ago and write it up on some darn 'form' or another.

Your CPD is the elephant in the room. The more you ignore it the bigger it gets.

You don't need to play catch-up. It really is hard work (see the box over-page for my confession).

So, what could be easier?

Why make CPD difficult?

- ✓ Devise a system along the lines suggested here.
- ✓ Keep it in mind as you go along.
- ✓ Realise that the journey (doing stuff) is more fun than the destination (a completed record)
- ✓ You'll have time to enjoy the finer things in life.

I was on holiday last summer when I noted an e-mail from my Regulator reminding me I had not submitted my online CPD record on time. They advised they were giving me a few weeks grace. Hurrah... so I went off to the beach!

A few weeks later I was on a train for Bristol to deliver a day's training when my PA called saying I'd been phoned by my Institute reminding me that I risked forfeiting my 'Chartered' status if I didn't submit my 1200 word report before midnight. Which file should she upload...?

OMG...

By Bristol I had worked out what they needed and had 150 words on my laptop. Over lunch another 200 or so words appeared.

I was now hungry and irritable.

On the evening train east I quickly realised I'd blown it.

Yike: if it wasn't for a delayed train out of Didcot Parkway as I sat on a windswept platform (the coffee shop had shut at 9 p.m.) I would not have made it...

Or I could have followed my own advice!

CHAPTER FOUR

PROFESSIONALISM – GETTING 'CLIENTS' NOT 'CUSTOMERS'

Clients appreciate your CPD – customers don't.

No surprise here: in my 20's I was an arrogant so-and-so[5]. Honours degree and a Post Grad, senior marketing position in Blue-Chip Pharma, managing my budgets to the penny and Industry Awards for my 'professionalism'. I thought I knew it all.

Two decades later I started my own firm, sole practitioner, so I went on a few courses: *'How to do PAYE'*, *'P11D's for Beginners'*, *'Company Taxation in a Minute'*, *'VAT for Dummies'* and *'Excise and Excuses'*. Being a geek I even invested in the *Which Guide to Tax* each year. I saved a fortune in accountant's fees. Sorted..!

After another decade I met the dad of one of the lads I coached at junior rugby – he asked who did my personal tax returns. *"Me? Alpha male, mate. I do my own"*.

(I thought, 'Why become a *customer* of an accountant as I know best?')

To cut a long story short, he reviewed my situation and gained me a £9,000 tax rebate for unclaimed expenses I didn't know about – and HMRC agreed with him, too[6]. (Yup, I became his client). Here's what I learnt:

✗ Customers – *they think they know best*

---

[5] I probably still am one!
[6] Accountants don't call, please. We are CLIENTS of his firm and they are still our accountants – although he is retired!

✓ Clients – *they know **you** know best*

That is what 'professionalism' is to me and I hope you have some empathy.

As a professional, you know that you are living in a 'knowledge economy'. And as you are engaged in 'cognitive' work, thinking, solving problems for people that rely on you to 'deliver a proper standard of service', people that come to you because *Google LLP* (or *Google QC*, *Google MRCVS* or *Dr Google*, etc.) can't help them. What you know is your leverage.

16 million+ people have watched Dan Pink[7] on YouTube explain that what professionals like you want from the workplace is to do something useful (purpose), have some freedom to do work your way (autonomy), and get better at stuff (mastery). Hence this book title: ***Master* your CPD**.

So, rather than have 'customers' who want the lowest price (they know best – they think) you'll want to attract clients that *value* your advice, so you'll want to develop and maintain that leading edge of knowledge (*mastery*). It is fun. And it shouldn't distract you from that core *purpose* of solving clients' problems.

Increased Professionalism (doing your CPD) = Increased value for your services = increased income for you

---

[7] *Drive: The surprising truth about what motivates us'*

CHAPTER FIVE

PROCESS – YOUR CPD IN 3 EASY STEPS

Let's get on and simplify the process of doing your CPD. Ask yourself three questions:

- ✓ **Step One**: What standard of competence do I need?
- ✓ **Step Two**: How do I compare to that standard?
- ✓ **Step Three**: What steps do I need to attain, maintain, or develop beyond that standard?

Let's answer your first question:

STEP ONE: WHAT STANDARD DO I NEED TO ATTAIN?

Lucky you – a professional often requires a pertinent academic attainment along with vocational (on the job) training. And at that point, the various Regulators define what 'competences' are required at the point of 'qualification', 'admission', 'day-one', and so on. Alternatively, you may choose to be a member of an Institute representing your profession. They have their defined standards, too.

All these can be viewed as a ***Threshold Standard at the point of qualification***: if you can't clear it, you shouldn't practice.

So, that is the minimum 'benchmark' against which you should compare. Which one is yours...?

SOLICITORS

On 11 March 2015, the SRA Board approved the publication of a **Competence Statement** *for solicitors. Made up of three parts (a statement of solicitor competence, the threshold standard and a statement of legal knowledge), the competence statement defines the continuing competences that we require from all solicitors.*

ACCOUNTANTS – THE ASSOCIATION OF CHARTERED CERTIFIED ACCOUNTANTS (ACCA)

The global body for professional accountants list their **Comprehensive Framework** on their webpages and I am not going to infringe their copyright by repeating it here. If you are interested, you'll find the detail online!

BARRISTERS

The **Professional Statement** *describes the knowledge, skills and attributes that all barristers will have on 'day one' of practice (i.e. upon the issue of a full qualification certificate, on which basis they may apply for a full practising certificate).*

Competences are defined for each knowledge, skill and attribute. Barristers should demonstrate all competences in order to evidence that they have met the requirements specified in the Professional Statement.

- *Legal knowledge and skills*
- *Advocacy*
- *Practice Management*
- *Working with clients and others*
- *Ethics, professionalism and judgement*

*The **Core Curriculum** statement is produced by the Royal College of General Practitioners (RCGP) which defines the learning outcomes for the specialty of general practice and describes the competences you require to practise medicine as a general practitioner in the National Health Service (NHS) of the United Kingdom. Although primarily aimed at the start of independent work as a general practitioner, it must also prepare the doctor beyond the training period and provide support for a professional life of development and change.*

VETERINARY SURGEONS – MEMBERS OF THE ROYAL COLLEGE OF VETERINARY SURGEONS

Rights and responsibilities go hand in hand. For this reason, on admission to membership of the RCVS, and in exchange for the right to practise veterinary surgery in the UK, every veterinary surgeon makes a declaration, which, since 1 April 2012, has been:

"I PROMISE AND SOLEMNLY DECLARE that I will pursue the work of my profession with integrity and accept my responsibilities to the public, my clients, the profession and the Royal College of Veterinary Surgeons, and that, ABOVE ALL, my constant endeavour will be to ensure the health and welfare of animals committed to my care."

From there, The **RCVS Code of Professional Conduct** sets out veterinary surgeons' professional responsibilities. Supporting guidance provides further advice on the proper standards of professional practice.

Under the ECPD[8] scheme, dentists will need to complete a minimum of 100 hours verifiable CPD over their five year cycle as well as ensuring they declare at least 10 hours during any 2 year period.

From 1 January 2018 all dentists will move on to the enhanced CPD scheme. Depending on where you are in your cycle you will have to complete CPD based on the current and new scheme to be compliant at the end of the cycle. A pro-rata approach will be applied and you will be able to find out how many hours you need to complete by using the transition tool. Once your current cycle ends, the CPD requirements for your next cycle will be based on the new scheme.

- *Dentist 2018-2022 – the new 5 year enhanced CPD cycle begins on 1 January 2018.*
- *Total number of hours required at the end of the 5-year cycle: 100 of which 100 must be verifiable.*
- *Don't forget you need to spread your CPD out over your cycle. With enhanced CPD you must complete at least 10 hours of verifiable CPD every two years.*

HOW TO MAKE SENSE OF THE STANDARD

Let's just clarify things a bit first. May I use what solicitors are expected to do to illustrate the approach?

Looking at the detail, and this equally applies to any professional, the 'Threshold Standard' at qualification (Level 3) of the Solicitors' Regulatory Authority Competency Framework, (states that) Solicitors should be able to:

A2 Maintain the level of competence and (technical) knowledge needed to practise effectively, taking into account changes in

---

[8] Enhanced CPD – from the UK General Dental Council

their role and/or practice context and developments in (technical aspects of their profession), including:

a) Taking responsibility for personal learning and development.

Well? Do you or don't you do that? See the problem: your answer is either yes or no!

[The other problem, who is this aimed at – it isn't speaking to you **directly**].

So, making life easy, you can turn each statement in the framework into the first person singular (**I**...), rephrase to make it more relevant to **you**, and rather than the yes/no answer you might prefer to consider the frequency with which you *do* these things: *never, sometimes, often, nearly always or always*?

Then the statement translates to:

o *I take responsibility to manage my own CPD opportunities appropriately as (add the technical aspects of my profession – law, accountancy, etc.) and my role develops*

And now it is easy to answer the ***frequency*** that you do this.

With this in mind, let's go on to look at how simple it can be for you to measure yourself against that standard for all your L&D...

CHAPTER SIX

PERFORMANCE – STEP 2: MEASURE THIS IN 3 MINUTES

When measuring your professional competence you will first need to decide what you do to manage your learning and development (L&D).

To do this simply, have a look at this straightforward template for the L&D competency sub-set:

This competency area encourages you to reflect on the degree to which you manage your own learning and development: from understanding your learning styles and exploring your options for learning and CPD.

Thinking about yourself at work, consider (i.e. reflect on) the regularity that you actually undertake each activity in practice – perhaps in the last couple of months – then record (✓) that frequency in the appropriate column:

Name: Date: / / *3. Maintain my competence, knowledge, L&D*	Never	Sometimes	Often	Nearly always	Always
I seek feedback from others (e.g. colleagues / clients) to enhance self-awareness of my performance					
I spot matters that are outside my expertise and take appropriate action					
I admit mistakes or recognise when I am experiencing difficulties and take appropriate corrective action					

... continue over page:

d)	I willingly share my experiences to help others in my workgroup develop to promote organisational learning				
e)	I recognise my preferred learning style(s) and actively develop varied approaches to maximise my opportunities to learn				
f)	I explore all options for my continuing professional development				
g)	I take responsibility to manage my own CPD opportunities appropriately as (technical aspects)and my role develops				
h)	I undertake the activities identified in my development plan promptly and evaluate their contribution to my performance				
Total – sum the number of your responses in each column					
Rating – multiply your column total above by this rating	0	1	2	3	4
Score – write your score for each column					
Sum your five scores – your total across all five columns					/32

From this reflection, define your next steps to improve or maintain your performance in each area:

> *Define your development goal and add this to your CPD record*

How long did it take you to complete the assessment?

Three minutes? In that time you explored a range of learning approaches, reflected on how frequently you do these things, and thought about what you might like to improve going forward.

EASY SELF-APPRAISAL AND APPRAISING OTHERS

Let us assume for a moment that you are not the most senior person in your firm – i.e. you have a boss!

In this case, the system works brilliantly for them, too.

As appraisee you are asked to consider (i.e. reflect on) the frequency with which you actually do each activity in practice – and your supervisor does the same reflecting on you, the appraisee.

To help them, the statements of any given competency can each be made easily into the third person, i.e.

This person: Takes responsibility to manage their own CPD opportunities appropriately as (technical aspects of their job) and their role develops

A simple template like the one for the appraisee can be made and they help structure conversations, such as annual appraisals, between you and your supervisor – although simple enough to be used more frequently than once a year.

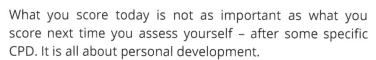

If your score is at some variance to your manager's, this will warrant further investigation.

So, if your mean score is less than, say, 80% attainment, it suggests that you may benefit from some form of CPD.

What you score today is not as important as what you score next time you assess yourself – after some specific CPD. It is all about personal development.

This may be an internal training course (run by a member of staff or using an external tutor), a public event from a CPD provider, or any of a dozen other activities – of which more later.

Once you have **_reflected_** on what you do, you are in a better position to **_plan_** what you need to do to develop professionally.

Incidentally, if you'd like to explore templates for yourself, your staff, and have a guide to running these easy-to-use approaches across 12 core competences of a professional, contact me for details of the **DAW CPD Tool Kit** (www.daw-cpd.com)

Turning to the range of non-technical skills of any professional, DAW have developed 12 sub-sets enabling you (and your boss) to reflect in the same way as above:

1. **Ethics, professionalism, sound judgment, confidentiality**

   o Ethical principles, code of conduct, respecting diversity and acting fairly…

2. **Apply understanding, critical thinking and analysis to solve problems**

   o Decision-making and risks, assessing information, problem solving …

3. **Managing own learning and development**

   o Understanding own learning styles, options for learning / CPD, learning needs analysis…

4. **Developing technical legal knowledge**

   o Research methods, effective use of questioning and active listening…

5. **Spoken and written advocacy** – *being able to represent your profession professionally*

   o Preparing, presenting a reasoned argument, countering

6. **Negotiating skills** – *dealing with clients and the others*

   o Planning, style, cooperation, persuasion, conflict, judgment...

7. **Professional relations with clients**

   o Dealing with client vulnerability, building confidence, professionalism...

8. **Professional relations with people in the firm**

   o Dealing with conflict, team working, delegating, supervising people...

9. **Managing performance**

   o Monitoring my own performance, monitoring others and the team

10. **Communicate effectively**

    o Clear, concise professional writing, zero tolerance in punctuation, presenting orally...

11. **Workload management and projects**

    o Initiate, plan, prioritise and manage work, records, confidentiality, security, data protection...

12. **Applying good business practice**

    o Organisation, finance in context, calculate and manage costs, billing, conduct issues...

Remember, just contact me for details of the **DAW CPD Tool Kit** (www.daw-cpd.com)

Naturally enough, there are more advanced standards as you progress your career – a **career path** for the various levels in your profession – but defined specifically for your firm.

That's where we help organisations write their own as obviously various businesses in the same sector are going to differ in so many ways – number of staff, type of work, ownership, and so on.

A mapped career path will be very handy if you want to recruit and retain the best talent.

Again, contact us if you want a guide to clarify your own: (www.daw-cpd.com).

CHAPTER SEVEN

PLAN – STEP 3: PLANNING YOUR PROGRESS

Poor Planning Produces Pretty Poor Performance!

Any unplanned training and development activity is very unlikely to bring the maximum return on your investment of time and money.

> *"We do not learn from experience... we learn from reflecting on that experience"*
> **John Dewey**

Best practice encourages all professionals to plan their training activity and to tie-in individual L&D needs with those of their practice to meet organisational objectives.

Anyone working in firms holding the Investors in People Award will be familiar with this approach.

The process starts with reflecting on what is needed.

WHAT IS MEANT BY REFLECTION?

It is what you did when you thought about your L&D needs using the Assessment Sheet in step 2 a moment ago.

You can do this any day – and it only takes around 3 minutes for each of 12 core competences of a professional. The sheets are in the **DAW CPD Tool Kit** (www.daw-cpd.com)

Here are some more thoughts on reflection:

Reflection means creating opportunities to step back from your practice to ask yourself (in three minutes):

- *How am I performing?*

- *What have I learned from my experience?*

- *What might I do differently in the future?*

Naturally enough, getting some feedback from other people that you work with will be useful in this reflective mode.

Note, you can reflect on your practice at:

- The 'general' level (e.g. considering your work generally or a particular type of job you do regularly).

- The 'transactional' level (i.e. reflecting on a specific matter that you are currently undertaking or have recently completed).

Reflection can also mean that you identify something that is happening or has happened during your work that you:

- Think you've done well (and which demonstrates your ongoing competence in your role), or

- Think you could have done better (and which, having reflected on it, you recognise how to go about doing better next time), or

- Think you could have done better (but which, having reflected on it, you are not sure how to go about doing better next time or that you cannot put right without some investigation on your own or some external help). Note: In this example, you have identified a 'development need'.

This approach is applicable to your skills (technical and so-called 'soft' skills) and your knowledge. You can keep your skills and knowledge up to date through a number of ways.

To help you think deeper about your work, you may want to ask yourself the following questions:

- *What am I good at (strengths) and what could I do better (development needs)?*

- *How could I have done a piece of work better?*

- *Was that to do with knowledge, technical skills or 'soft' skills / behaviours?*

    - o *If so, what knowledge, skills or behaviours were lacking?*

- *In relation to that knowledge, or those skills or behaviours, how would I describe where I am now compared to where I need to be?*

- *What do I need to do to get to where I need to be?*

This can be simply recorded on a couple of sheets of paper – covered in Section 9 ('Proof').

WHAT SORT OF ACTIVITY (LEARNING APPROACH) SUITS YOU BEST?

David Kolb published his learning styles model in 1984 from which he developed his learning style inventory. His theory works on two levels: a four-stage cycle of learning and four separate learning styles.

Kolb states that learning involves the acquisition of abstract concepts that can be applied flexibly in a range of situations. In Kolb's theory, the impetus for the development of new concepts is provided by new experiences.

Much of his theory is concerned with your internal thinking (cognitive) processes.

Kolb observed that people appear to go through a 'learning cycle'; this is where you:

(a) have an experience
(b) reflect on that experience
(c) draw some conclusions from that reflection
(d) plan how to be more effective in that situation next time it occurs

Kolb suggests that those who travel around the cycle regularly are most likely to maximise their learning, and thus become more effective.

He also observes, however, that for most people, one or more parts of the cycle are not undertaken at all, or not carried out very well.

Progressing this idea, it is suggested that there are four different **Styles of Learning**, largely corresponding to the four points of Kolb's cycle. The four Styles are described as:

(a) **Activists** – who generally learn by doing, and activity

(b) **Reflectors** – who generally learn by watching, and thinking

(c) **Theorists** – who learn by reading to understand basic concepts

(d) **Pragmatists** – who learn by finding relevance and practical applications

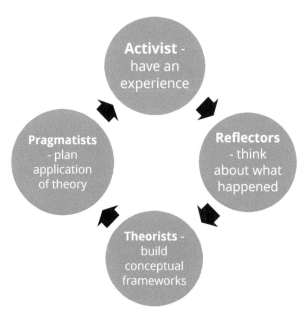

Learning is a joined up process with each stage being mutually supportive of and feeding into the next.

It is possible to enter the cycle at any stage and follow it through its logical sequence.

However, experience suggests that the most effective learning occurs when you can execute all four stages of the model. Therefore, no one stage of the cycle is as effective as a learning procedure on its own.

The Learning Styles Questionnaire (from Honey & Mumford) can guide you on an indication of your own current preferences in the balance of the four styles. It can, therefore, suggest to you potential preferences or possible less favourable approaches in your own learning habits, upon which this understanding can be used to build your professional development.

Contact me if you'd like some support to uncover your learning preferences: (www.daw-cpd.com)

Your learning activity can then be specifically devised to assist in developing personal learning across the four styles, encouraging frequent passes around Kolb's Cycle, for example:

Training Courses may offer:
- *practical activities to strengthen and call upon your* **Activist** *style*
- *individual exercises followed by discussions, to strengthen and call upon your powers of* **Reflection**
- *case studies and real work applications, to strengthen and call upon* **Pragmatic** *approaches*

Workbooks or handy Booklets, like this one you are reading now, offer:
- *practical activities, often with workplace application for you to reflect upon (***Activist, Pragmatist, Reflector***)*
- *ideas from management researchers and visionaries, to help you understand and build concepts (***Theorist***)*
- *prompts for discussions with others (***Pragmatist, Reflector***)*

Textbooks offer:
- *food for thought (***Reflection***)*
- *key ideas from research and writings (***Theorist***)*

Discussion with your manager offers:
- *potential for new, expanded, or developing* **Activities** *in the workplace*
- **Reflection** *in discussion with supporters*
- *drawing out of Concepts and Principles (***Theorist***)*
- *potential for* **Pragmatic** *applications of theories*

Assessment activities, such as the L&D Assessment Sheets in the DAW CPD Tool Kit, offer:
- *real workplace investigative* **Activity**
- **Reflection** *on the effectiveness of current practises and processes*

- *exploration of **Theoretical** concepts appropriate to a given topic area*
- *Application of ideas and concepts to real workplace situations (**Pragmatist**)*

Travelling round the cycle, using all four Styles effectively, should maximise your learning, both from formal training, and in the workplace.

Having done the first step (where am I now – professionally), secondly answer a handful of substantive questions based on your reflection and planned use of your preferred learning style(s):

a) *What do I need or want to learn?*
b) *What activities will best achieve the learning outcomes I seek?*
c) *Who will support me or what resources do I need?*
d) *How will I know I have achieved success?*
e) *What is my target date for review?*

From there, you can set personal objectives over the short (next month), medium (over the next quarter), and longer term (year-end). Make sure that these goals are 'SMART':

- **Specific** – detailed enough to be clear and concise, e.g.
  - *Learn about the fee estimate planning process...*
- **Measurable** – so that you know when they are done, e.g.
  - *...so that I can take on this task for all clients...*
- **Achievable** – not so easy they don't present a challenge
- **Relevant** – it matters to you and what you are being paid to do: your competences!
- **Time-bound** – so you know by when they have to be completed, e.g.
  - *...by the end of this quarter Q2*

One way of capturing this information is through a Personal Development Plan (PDP). Such a record contains information that enables you to demonstrate that you have taken appropriate steps to maintain your competence and provide a proper standard of service. While your regulator may not prescribe a specific approach, for each of your identified L&D need(s) you may find it useful to record:

- *what you did;*
- *how it was related to ensuring your competence;*
- *what you learnt;*
- *when the activity was completed.*

It may be appropriate for you to continue to capture L&D using your organisation's existing systems or adapting them to capture this information. Section 9 ('Proof') shows you how to do this quickly and easily.

You can evaluate the effectiveness of L&D activity you have completed by simply thinking about what you have learnt and considering whether it has met your identified need or whether you need to undertake further activity.

This process is important; it will help you understand if further L&D is required to help you achieve what you set out to learn. It may also highlight new L&D needs that you were not previously aware of. Adopting this approach can help to ensure that you remain competent to provide a proper standard of service.

If you feel that the activity undertaken has satisfied your L&D need, then you can record this information. If it did not, or new needs have emerged, then you need to think about how you plan to address them.

This can then be converted into a simple form (Sheet 2 – your plan) for your records. So, in summary:

A.   First: Assess your learning needs and summarise on your SWOT – Sheet 1, see Section 9 'Proof' – one sheet of A4
B.   Next: Define your learning Goals – see above
C.   Finally: Write your PLAN – Sheet 2, devise your own using the template in Section 9 ('Proof) – your second sheet of A4...

CHAPTER EIGHT

PLEASURE – 12 FUN THINGS TO DO (... THAT YOU PROBABLY DO ALREADY)

The options you have to get better at stuff are many and varied; which works best for you may depend on your favoured learning style (see earlier) but would include:

- **Traditional training courses** – in-house in your firm or an open course from one of the CPD providers – perhaps attend an industry conference. Remember, e-learning (webinars, courses, podcasts, online articles) also count as CPD – and DAW has a growing portfolio specifically developed to match your soft-skills competences.

  Why not join our monthly webinar programme to build your professional portfolio of 'soft skills'? (www.daw-cpd.com)

- **Shared learning** – where someone attends a course then delivers edited highlights back at the firm.
- **Informal learning** – where each approach has its pros and cons.
  1) traditionally *'master and servant'* where one shares an office with someone more senior that has the skills to help you improve but that can be distracting for both parties unless carefully managed.

2) ***Research, reading***, journals, etc. provided it is focused on your needs then it can be very useful and time-effective. Too busy or bushed to read more at the end of the day – download  my podcasts and have a listen on your commute home! (www.daw-cpd.com)

3) ***Assigned reading*** – defined by your supervisor can be more effective provided again that it is focused on your specific needs.

4) ***'Targeted' research, reading and discussion*** – when based on clear L&D needs, perhaps in the context of a given matter – and discussed with a colleague – it can help develop further understanding.

5) ***Colleagues*** – this should be encouraged in a truly 'learning organisation'. Working on committees / panels / discussion groups are also good L&D opportunities.

6) ***External peers*** – the external perspective can be very insightful.

7) ***Networking*** – used to address identified L&D needs, be they around knowledge, skills or identifying good practice. Naturally, you'll need the network in the first place! (See also Social media below).

8) ***Regional L&D hubs*** – larger professional service firms provide resources for you to address your L&D needs. These networks may be appropriate for smaller firms or sole practitioners and typically involve the larger firm providing L&D in return for referrals of work the smaller firm is not in a position to handle.

9) **Coaching** – this involves a dialogue, based on L&D needs, where the coach helps an individual to develop their own action points to address identified goals and objectives. Watch out for our online programme!

10) **Mentoring** – informal or defined schemes these 1-2-1 sessions can provide ongoing support, encouragement, advice and feedback on work and more 'pastoral' or career development advice. This can be very effective – watch out for details of my special programme!

11) **Secondments** – mostly the preserve of the larger organisation, secondments involve a temporary movement of an employee to another part of an organisation or to an external (maybe client / supplier) organisation for a defined period and provide exposure to environments and situations that can help address L&D needs.

12) **Social media** – being selective about what and who you follow can be a great source of ideas, information, experiences and views – consider some of the **LinkedIn** *Interest Groups*. **Twitter** has specific groups for you to follow. When focused, it can be a cost effective way to address gaps in your knowledge.

CHAPTER NINE

PROOF – RECORDING YOUR CPD AND EVIDENCE

Remember what we said in section 2.7 about how your clever brain remembers what you write by hand – when you become the author of what you create!

I know online learning management systems (LMS) are a crucial part of what organisations need to track who has done what. After all, there are significant pieces of legislation anyone at any work-place must know and apply to ensure the proper running of the organisation: health & safety, discrimination at work, compliance, money laundering, cybercrime, bribery... and so the list goes on. And crucial these things are, too.

I work with some of the foremost LMS providers and have helped them improve their systems.

But that is about the organisation. I'd like to help you – as an individual. Re-read section 2.7 and consider the following two sheets of A4 you can keep to hand, update, change, re-write, colour, sketch, and make another version in minutes.

Oh, and you will help the ideas stick in your higher cognitive brain (the prefrontal cortex).

With all your reflection that has been going on, it will be useful to summarise where you are now.

One of the simplest ways of doing that is to undertake a personal SWOT analysis: an acronym for your strengths / weaknesses / opportunities / threats. This exercise can be repeated annually / quarterly – or as often as you feel necessary as you work through your competency Assessment Sheets and professional learning.

Advice for Dentists from the General Dental Council is one example:

Your PDP can be created individually or in conjunction with your peers, your employer / line manager / commissioner or your wider dental team. Many health professionals find it useful to work with a mentor to develop their learning needs, and the GDC encourages you to build this kind of relationship where possible.

One sheet of A4 paper might look like:

Name:	Date: / /
Things that I do well: *Strengths*	**Things that I could do better:** *Weaknesses*
1. My personal administration on the client files and basic skills are good and my technical knowledge is generally sound for my level of experience.	*1. My understanding of the fee estimate planning process is still superficial in places (too many invoice queries) and requires more clarity.*
2.	*2.*
Things that will help me: *Opportunities*	**Things that might hinder me:** *Threats*
1. I can call on the support of my line manager to give me guidance on personal development.	*1. Balancing work and personal commitments*
2.	*2.*

Nothing too complicated; you know where you are, where you are going, what will help you get there and what the obstacles might be. And updated in 3 minutes.

Having 'slept on it', then you might firm up your goals the next day. And because you are busy with your main work demands – clients / patients and the like – you know that a structured approach to your L&D plans will save you precious time.

MY CPD PLAN – SHEET TWO

So, the next step is a highly focused plan of activity closely matched to your assessment of those key competency areas.

This is called a Professional Development Plan: you are a professional so why wouldn't you use one.

Have a look at my version and adapt it to suit you – just on one other A4 sheet of paper.

Continuing Professional Development Plan Example				DAW
Name: *Peter Sample*		**Covering Period**		
Firm: *DAW Law LLP*		**From:** *1st Oct 2016*		**To:** *31st Dec 2016*
Membership Number: *01295 768606*				
Competency Group "What"	Current Assessment / TNA "Reflection"	Where do I need to be? "Goal"	How will I get there? "Plan"	When completed + assessment of activity to my CPD? "Done"
3. Maintain my Competence, Knowledge, Learning & Development	95% ave. of self & supervisor: - Unrecognised learning style - Missed opportunities to learn from team	Recognise opportunities to stay current with developments in legal practice making best use of preferred learning style by end of this quarter	Use Honey & Mumford learning style questionnaire - CPD Course. Discuss opportunities with workgroup and supervisor at monthly meeting. Attend to defined reading from supervisor; schedule 2hrs. each week	Reflector / Theorist Style favours more reading and listening to other's experiences; now attending to both reading and group discussions *This is giving me more confidence when approaching more complex matters* Any further action? More of the same - better scheduled!

© DAW Ltd. (2016)   Not for commercial use   www.dawlaw.co.uk

Pre-pared blanks are in the **DAW CPD Tool Kit**, (www.daw-cpd.com)

52

To demonstrate compliance make sure your skills and knowledge remain up to date; your regulator expects you to demonstrate this if called up to do so. These two sheets of A4, and their various versions, in a folder in your desk or online, are proof.

But that is not the only reason why you develop yourself as a professional.

As a professional, meeting the competences set out in your profession's Competence Statement forms an integral part of the requirement to provide a proper standard of service to your clients and is a minimum. Striving further than that is the mark of a *true* professional.

So, in summary

1. **Reflect** on the quality of what you do by reference to your profession's Competence Statement to identify individual specific L&D needs. The Competence Statement is generic and so all professionals will need to apply it to their practice. Summarise that on a SWOT – one sheet of A4.

   The assessment example used in this guide is one way.

2. **Plan** and **address** your L&D needs. The structure offered here is one way.

3. **Record** and **evaluate** your learning activity so that, if your regulator needed to engage with you on a specific matter or where they have evidence of a competence risk, you can demonstrate to them that you have taken steps to ensure your ongoing competence. Your Personal Development Plan (PDP) is the other A4 sheet.

   Failure to demonstrate that you have reflected on the quality of your practice and addressed any L&D needs, may be an aggravating factor in disciplinary action they may take.

Demonstrating your CPD attainment to your Professional Indemnity underwriter may help keep your premiums in check.

4. Make an **annual declaration** to confirm you have completed the above. You can find more information on how to complete your profession's declaration in the usual way.

FOR EMPLOYERS

Employers are responsible for delivering a proper standard of service to their clients and for training their staff to maintain a level of competence appropriate to their work and level of responsibility. Firms may want to consider how this booklet's resources align with your current approach to L&D so that you continue to meet this obligation.

CHAPTER TEN

PRACTICAL SOLUTION – DAW CPD TOOL KIT

Professionals faced with the challenge of taking a 'reflective approach' to CPD under their professions' regimen need to look no further. To aid organisations in establishing the new approach DAW have put their heads together and developed a comprehensive support package to guide professionals and their managers through the process.

The **DAW CPD Tool Kit** contains:

1. Professional Manager Discussion Notes – the introductory discussion notes that aim to steer managers and supervisors through the process and offers a step-by-step guide to having conversations with staff about their CPD plans.

SECTION 1

2. Learning Needs Analysis (LNA) – blank forms to help professionals reflect on their activity at work in 12 areas or 'soft skills' matched against the Competency Framework for most qualified professionals – the 'Threshold Standard'.

SECTION 2

3. Manager LNA forms – a similar set of forms in the same 12 areas to help managers and supervisors assess the competences of each member of their professional staff. DAW have incorporated all the key 'soft' Competences but avoided duplication – and added a couple of others – particularly on financials!

SECTION 3

4. Learning & Development Checklist – a range of options to guide all staff on alternative CPD activities to help them develop their competences.

5. Recording your CPD – a guide for staff to help explain how they can record their CPD.

6. My Personal Audit: S.W.O.T. – a simple one-page template to help staff summarise their situation at any given time.

7. Continuing Professional Development Plan – a one-page template for staff to record their CPD goals, actions and note of completion.

SECTION 4

8. Staff Appraisal Competence Summary – a single sheet for managers to record each person's CPD attainment across all 12 competences and their progress, helping managers and supervisors focus on the development needs of their team.

SECTION 5

9. CPD Workshop Booking Form – a single document to help book specific training needs.

10. Workshop: 'Managing my Learning & Development' – example outline of an online webinar workshop to guide your people.

11. Career Path Document – section of generic examples to show the growing complexity in developing competences framework.

12. Loyalty Vouchers – discounting your investment in the DAW fees for online webinar membership packages of 12 CPD training events.

The pack contents can be reproduced internally as many times as you need for all managers and all their professional staff – but may not be used commercially (sold on to another).

This comprehensive resource is currently listed at £249.50 (+VAT) – yes, less than a fiver a week.

To find out how to make it work for you, or to place an order, please use the contact form at www.daw-cpd.com or email advice@daw.co.uk

We'll show you how to use the tool kit

Write your own notes here...
 – *you become the author of what you read*

Write your own notes here...
  – *you become the author of what you read*

ABOUT THE AUTHOR

Mac is a Chartered Marketer and a Chartered Manager specialising in advising organisations on management and marketing, with experience of people at all levels.

While very well qualified in his disciplines, Mac has a knack of making the complex appear simple, the theory work in practice, and creates both entertaining as well as effective learning experiences.

His passion is transferring his knowledge and experience to others to enable their work to become more fulfilling.

Authorship

A writer for professional journals, he co-authored *"Below-the-Line Promotion"* (1992), the *"Fundamentals of Advertising, 2nd Ed"* (1999), and *"The Fundamentals and Practice of Marketing 4th Ed."* (2002) with John Wilmshurst and is Editor of the 5th Edition of *The Practice of Advertising* (2004). He is sole author of *"Motivation, Ability & Confidence Building in People"* and *"Recruiting, Retaining & Releasing People"* (2007).

Education

An Honours graduate from Leeds University, he holds a Diploma in Marketing, a Masters' Degree (MBA) in Strategic Marketing and was elected a full Member of the Chartered Management Institute. He was awarded a Postgraduate Certificate in Management from Northampton University and accredited Chartered Manager (since 2012) and Chartered Marketer (since 1994). He achieved a CAM Diploma in Digital Marketing from Oxford College (2014).

Pastoral

Mac is married to Jan and they have the good fortune to share five children. He has coached junior rugby, is a former RFU Society Referee, an 'advanced motorcyclist', and 'over-the-hill' jogger. He enjoys reviewing his personal collection of sea-shells that remain on public display on the beaches of the world...